H. Frederick

Affirm

Alivia Hendershot

© 2019 by John F. Hendershot
All rights reserved. This book or any portion thereof may not be reproduced or used in any manner whatsoever without the express written permission of the publisher except for the use of brief quotations in a book review.
ISBN: 9781075936319

Goal Setting:

In our lives it is necessary to have goals that we are in progress of attaining in an effort to strengthen our character, work ethic, but to also challenge us to become better in various areas of our lives.

Real success in life is rarely an accident. There are intentional benchmarks set from everything from getting good grades, becoming great at a task, sport, or endeavor.

Greatness is a process that can take years, decades, and even lifetimes to manifest the vision in which you were perusing. Hopefully, the process doesn't dissuade you from your dreams and goals and that you develop the resolve to keep moving forward through life's sometimes more challenging times.

This book is designed to assist you in becoming intentional about looking forward and setting goals that have the possibility to allow you to live an extraordinary life full of purpose, and meaning.

To many of us fail to live intentionally squandering the great gift that we are afforded for such a small amount of time. Our lives are vastly important, as we have an opportunity to bring hope and resources to others throughout within our hurting world.

You have an opportunity to become a transformational leader, but part of your responsibility as an emerging leader is to prepare yourself by becoming a disciplined goal setter and achiever. Take heart that though this process is difficult it equips you with a skill that very few individuals successfully attain therefore underlying how important it is to develop this valuable skill in generations to come.

I want to affirm that anyone is capable of achieving this discipline, and I want to commend you for taking the first step in acquiring this skill by opening this book.

In the pages ahead, I want you to start with goals that are smaller in nature, and allow yourself to opportunity to slowly become conditioned with a mindset that understands the importance of intentional living and goal setting.

Those that master the discipline of goal setting will have an undeniable advantage on even the most gifted individuals that neglect to properly gain discipline through repetition of goal setting, and being willing to challenge themselves both mentally and physically.

You are the exception already, so now cultivate the discipline by using these guidelines in setting your goals.

1. Goals must be realistic, and attainable.
2. Goals must be specific in nature.
3. Goals must have the capability of being measurable.
4. Goals must be time specific.

In order to effectively meet your goal once you have defined it, you must define an action plan that incorporates the above four points.

I wish you great success in becoming a world class goal setter and achiever. I believe that you are capable of immensely more than you can ever fathom. Believe in yourself, and don't become frustrated when you stumble, but get back up quickly and begin again.

You matter; your life matter, and you were destined for greatness!

Your Friend,

John F. Hendershot

Examples of how to plan your Goals:

1. Test your skill level against the goal to obtain measurable points.
2. Obtain insights from others who have successfully achieved the goal that you have set for yourself.
3. Through insight, and self-evaluation set a realistic timeframe to complete your goal.
4. Develop a plan of action that aligns with the timeframe that allows for progressive achievement through consistent "practice".
5. Consistent documentation that evaluates your progression through "practice" compared with the insights obtained through your research against your planned timeframe.
6. Goal completion
7. Celebrate your success

The GOAL

Your Goal Plan

What are three short-term goals that you have? (short-term = less than 6 months)

1. I wand to ern muney so I con by a things ~~di b it~~
2. T wand to take care of Eddie avey day
3. Clen avery day

Why are these goals important to you?

Goal #1 wen I get older People dot nedd to tell my wat to do

Goal #2 because Eddie my dog

Goal #3 So I no How to Clen

Are these goals realistic and attainable?

Who can you consult that has achieved these goals?

Have you conducted any research on attaining the goals?

Are the goals attainable within a six-month timeframe?

Have you developed an action plan?

Game Plan for Goal #1

Goal: _____

Expert Consult: _____

Relevant Advice from Expert Consultant:

Relevant Information from research conducted:

Goal Completion Time frame:

Action Plan:

1.

2.

3.

4.

Measurement/ Documentation of Goal:

Progression Notes:

Setbacks:

What did I learn?

Did I meet the expectations I set myself?

How has the Goal impacted my life?

Game Plan for Goal #2

Goal: _____

Expert Consult: _____

Relevant Advice from Expert Consultant:

Relevant Information from research conducted:

Goal Completion Time frame:

Action Plan:

1.

2.

3.

4.

Measurement/ Documentation of Goal:

Progression Notes:

Setbacks:

What did I learn?

Did I meet the expectations I set myself?

How has the Goal impacted my life?

Game Plan for Goal #3

Goal: _____

Expert Consult: _____

Relevant Advice from Expert Consultant:

Relevant Information from research conducted:

Goal Completion Time frame:

Action Plan:

1.

2.

3.

4.

Measurement/ Documentation of Goal:

Progression Notes:

Setbacks:

What did I learn?

Did I meet the expectations I set myself?

How has the Goal impacted my life?

Your Goal Plan

What are three long-term goals that you have? (long-term = 6-18 months)

1.

2.

3.

Why are these goals important to you?

Goal #1

Goal #2

Goal #3

Are these goals realistic and attainable?

Who can you consult that has achieved these goals?

Have you conducted any research on attaining the goals?

Are the goals attainable within a six-month timeframe?

Have you developed an action plan?

Game Plan for Goal #1

Goal: _____

Expert Consult: _____

Relevant Advice from Expert Consultant:

Relevant Information from research conducted:

Goal Completion Time frame:

Action Plan:

1.

2.

3.

4.

Measurement/ Documentation of Goal:

Progression Notes:

Setbacks:

What did I learn?

Did I meet the expectations I set myself?

How has the Goal impacted my life?

Game Plan for Goal #2

Goal: _____

Expert Consult: _____

Relevant Advice from Expert Consultant:

Relevant Information from research conducted:

Goal Completion Time frame:

Action Plan:

1.

2.

3.

4.

Measurement/ Documentation of Goal:

Progression Notes:

Setbacks:

What did I learn?

Did I meet the expectations I set myself?

How has the Goal impacted my life?

Game Plan for Goal #3

Goal: _____

Expert Consult: _____

Relevant Advice from Expert Consultant:

Relevant Information from research conducted:

Goal Completion Time frame:

Action Plan:

1.

2.

3.

4.

Measurement/ Documentation of Goal:

Progression Notes:

Setbacks:

What did I learn?

Did I meet the expectations I set myself?

How has the Goal impacted my life?

Affirmation Journal

I am confident

Today's Date: July 5 2019
Time: 9:30 Pm
Writing from:

What Goal did I work on today? No toking Boke

I am proud of myself today because: I DiD a fole costr even no i was sleeopy

I really did well at Being Poshit today.

My goal for tomorrow is: To cling did it

What did I learn today? evne tow thet its a sort ride it tack a log time to wate

Other Notes:

I am strong

Today's Date: July 6 2019

Time: 9:27

Writing from:

What Goal did I work on today?

I am proud of myself today because:

I really did well at _____ today.

My goal for tomorrow is:

What did I learn today?

Other Notes:

I am whole

Today's Date:

Time:

Writing from:

What Goal did I work on today?

I am proud of myself today because:

I really did well at _____ today.

My goal for tomorrow is:

What did I learn today?

Other Notes:

I am a hard-worker

Today's Date:

Time:

Writing from:

What Goal did I work on today?

I am proud of myself today because:

I really did well at _____ today.

My goal for tomorrow is:

What did I learn today?

Other Notes:

I am persistent

Today's Date:

Time:

Writing from:

What Goal did I work on today?

I am proud of myself today because:

I really did well at _____ today.

My goal for tomorrow is:

What did I learn today?

Other Notes:

I am smart

Today's Date:

Time:

Writing from:

What Goal did I work on today?

I am proud of myself today because:

I really did well at _____ **today.**

My goal for tomorrow is:

What did I learn today?

Other Notes:

I am wise

Today's Date:

Time:

Writing from:

What Goal did I work on today?

I am proud of myself today because:

I really did well at _____ today.

My goal for tomorrow is:

What did I learn today?

Other Notes:

I make healthy choices

Today's Date:

Time:

Writing from:

What Goal did I work on today?

I am proud of myself today because:

I really did well at _____ today.

My goal for tomorrow is:

What did I learn today?

Other Notes:

I exceed expectations

Today's Date:

Time:

Writing from:

What Goal did I work on today?

I am proud of myself today because:

I really did well at _____ today.

My goal for tomorrow is:

What did I learn today?

Other Notes:

I am kind

Today's Date:

Time:

Writing from:

What Goal did I work on today?

I am proud of myself today because:

I really did well at _____ today.

My goal for tomorrow is:

What did I learn today?

Other Notes:

I am helpful

Today's Date:

Time:

Writing from:

What Goal did I work on today?

I am proud of myself today because:

I really did well at _____ **today.**

My goal for tomorrow is:

What did I learn today?

Other Notes:

I am selfless

Today's Date:

Time:

Writing from:

What Goal did I work on today?

I am proud of myself today because:

I really did well at _____ today.

My goal for tomorrow is:

What did I learn today?

Other Notes:

I am honest

Today's Date:

Time:

Writing from:

What Goal did I work on today?

I am proud of myself today because:

I really did well at _____ today.

My goal for tomorrow is:

What did I learn today?

Other Notes:

I am disciplined

Today's Date:

Time:

Writing from:

What Goal did I work on today?

I am proud of myself today because:

I really did well at _____ today.

My goal for tomorrow is:

What did I learn today?

Other Notes:

I am organized

Today's Date:

Time:

Writing from:

What Goal did I work on today?

I am proud of myself today because:

I really did well at _____ today.

My goal for tomorrow is:

What did I learn today?

Other Notes:

I am an original

Today's Date:

Time:

Writing from:

What Goal did I work on today?

I am proud of myself today because:

I really did well at _____ today.

My goal for tomorrow is:

What did I learn today?

Other Notes:

I am a problem solver

Today's Date:

Time:

Writing from:

What Goal did I work on today?

I am proud of myself today because:

I really did well at _____ today.

My goal for tomorrow is:

What did I learn today?

Other Notes:

I have vision

Today's Date:

Time:

Writing from:

What Goal did I work on today?

I am proud of myself today because:

I really did well at _____ today.

My goal for tomorrow is:

What did I learn today?

Other Notes:

I am loved

Today's Date:

Time:

Writing from:

What Goal did I work on today?

I am proud of myself today because:

I really did well at _____ **today.**

My goal for tomorrow is:

What did I learn today?

Other Notes:

I am polite

Today's Date:

Time:

Writing from:

What Goal did I work on today?

I am proud of myself today because:

I really did well at _____ today.

My goal for tomorrow is:

What did I learn today?

Other Notes:

I am professional

Today's Date:

Time:

Writing from:

What Goal did I work on today?

I am proud of myself today because:

I really did well at _____ today.

My goal for tomorrow is:

What did I learn today?

Other Notes:

I am well dressed

Today's Date:

Time:

Writing from:

What Goal did I work on today?

I am proud of myself today because:

I really did well at _____ today.

My goal for tomorrow is:

What did I learn today?

Other Notes:

I am creative

Today's Date:

Time:

Writing from:

What Goal did I work on today?

I am proud of myself today because:

I really did well at _____ today.

My goal for tomorrow is:

What did I learn today?

Other Notes:

I am punctual

Today's Date:

Time:

Writing from:

What Goal did I work on today?

I am proud of myself today because:

I really did well at _____ today.

My goal for tomorrow is:

What did I learn today?

Other Notes:

I am prepared

Today's Date:

Time:

Writing from:

What Goal did I work on today?

I am proud of myself today because:

I really did well at _____ today.

My goal for tomorrow is:

What did I learn today?

Other Notes:

I am respectful

Today's Date:

Time:

Writing from:

What Goal did I work on today?

I am proud of myself today because:

I really did well at _____ **today.**

My goal for tomorrow is:

What did I learn today?

Other Notes:

I love learning

Today's Date:

Time:

Writing from:

What Goal did I work on today?

I am proud of myself today because:

I really did well at _____ today.

My goal for tomorrow is:

What did I learn today?

Other Notes:

I am clam

Today's Date:

Time:

Writing from:

What Goal did I work on today?

I am proud of myself today because:

I really did well at _____ today.

My goal for tomorrow is:

What did I learn today?

Other Notes:

I am healthy

Today's Date:

Time:

Writing from:

What Goal did I work on today?

I am proud of myself today because:

I really did well at _____ today.

My goal for tomorrow is:

What did I learn today?

Other Notes:

I am worthy

Today's Date:

Time:

Writing from:

What Goal did I work on today?

I am proud of myself today because:

I really did well at _____ today.

My goal for tomorrow is:

What did I learn today?

Other Notes:

I accept my flaws

Today's Date:

Time:

Writing from:

What Goal did I work on today?

I am proud of myself today because:

I really did well at _____ today.

My goal for tomorrow is:

What did I learn today?

Other Notes:

I forgive myself

Today's Date:

Time:

Writing from:

What Goal did I work on today?

I am proud of myself today because:

I really did well at _____ **today.**

My goal for tomorrow is:

What did I learn today?

Other Notes:

I include others

Today's Date:

Time:

Writing from:

What Goal did I work on today?

I am proud of myself today because:

I really did well at _____ today.

My goal for tomorrow is:

What did I learn today?

Other Notes:

I respect my body

Today's Date:

Time:

Writing from:

What Goal did I work on today?

I am proud of myself today because:

I really did well at _____ **today.**

My goal for tomorrow is:

What did I learn today?

Other Notes:

I am grateful

Today's Date:

Time:

Writing from:

What Goal did I work on today?

I am proud of myself today because:

I really did well at _____ today.

My goal for tomorrow is:

What did I learn today?

Other Notes:

I love my family

Today's Date:

Time:

Writing from:

What Goal did I work on today?

I am proud of myself today because:

I really did well at _____ today.

My goal for tomorrow is:

What did I learn today?

Other Notes:

I belong

Today's Date:

Time:

Writing from:

What Goal did I work on today?

I am proud of myself today because:

I really did well at _____ today.

My goal for tomorrow is:

What did I learn today?

Other Notes:

I am a good friend

Today's Date:

Time:

Writing from:

What Goal did I work on today?

I am proud of myself today because:

I really did well at _____ today.

My goal for tomorrow is:

What did I learn today?

Other Notes:

I am trustworthy

Today's Date:

Time:

Writing from:

What Goal did I work on today?

I am proud of myself today because:

I really did well at _____ today.

My goal for tomorrow is:

What did I learn today?

Other Notes:

I am always learning

Today's Date:

Time:

Writing from:

What Goal did I work on today?

I am proud of myself today because:

I really did well at _____ **today.**

My goal for tomorrow is:

What did I learn today?

Other Notes:

I enjoy being challenged

Today's Date:

Time:

Writing from:

What Goal did I work on today?

I am proud of myself today because:

I really did well at _____ today.

My goal for tomorrow is:

What did I learn today?

Other Notes:

My mind is free from worry

Today's Date:

Time:

Writing from:

What Goal did I work on today?

I am proud of myself today because:

I really did well at _____ today.

My goal for tomorrow is:

What did I learn today?

Other Notes:

My words have power

Today's Date:

Time:

Writing from:

What Goal did I work on today?

I am proud of myself today because:

I really did well at _____ today.

My goal for tomorrow is:

What did I learn today?

Other Notes:

I peacefully resolve conflicts

Today's Date:

Time:

Writing from:

What Goal did I work on today?

I am proud of myself today because:

I really did well at _____ **today.**

My goal for tomorrow is:

What did I learn today?

Other Notes:

I ask for help when I need it

Today's Date:

Time:

Writing from:

What Goal did I work on today?

I am proud of myself today because:

I really did well at _____ today.

My goal for tomorrow is:

What did I learn today?

Other Notes:

I have good ideas

Today's Date:

Time:

Writing from:

What Goal did I work on today?

I am proud of myself today because:

I really did well at _____ **today.**

My goal for tomorrow is:

What did I learn today?

Other Notes:

My life matters

Today's Date:

Time:

Writing from:

What Goal did I work on today?

I am proud of myself today because:

I really did well at _____ today.

My goal for tomorrow is:

What did I learn today?

Other Notes:

I can

Today's Date:

Time:

Writing from:

What Goal did I work on today?

I am proud of myself today because:

I really did well at _____ today.

My goal for tomorrow is:

What did I learn today?

Other Notes:

I have people who care for me

Today's Date:

Time:

Writing from:

What Goal did I work on today?

I am proud of myself today because:

I really did well at _____ today.

My goal for tomorrow is:

What did I learn today?

Other Notes:

I am happy to be here

Today's Date:

Time:

Writing from:

What Goal did I work on today?

I am proud of myself today because:

I really did well at _____ today.

My goal for tomorrow is:

What did I learn today?

Other Notes:

I accept and love the way I look

Today's Date:

Time:

Writing from:

What Goal did I work on today?

I am proud of myself today because:

I really did well at _____ today.

My goal for tomorrow is:

What did I learn today?

Other Notes:

My opinion matters

Today's Date:

Time:

Writing from:

What Goal did I work on today?

I am proud of myself today because:

I really did well at _____ today.

My goal for tomorrow is:

What did I learn today?

Other Notes:

I see beauty in everything

Today's Date:

Time:

Writing from:

What Goal did I work on today?

I am proud of myself today because:

I really did well at _____ today.

My goal for tomorrow is:

What did I learn today?

Other Notes:

I can learn hard things

Today's Date:

Time:

Writing from:

What Goal did I work on today?

I am proud of myself today because:

I really did well at _____ today.

My goal for tomorrow is:

What did I learn today?

Other Notes:

I am compassionate

Today's Date:

Time:

Writing from:

What Goal did I work on today?

I am proud of myself today because:

I really did well at _____ today.

My goal for tomorrow is:

What did I learn today?

Other Notes:

I am protected

Today's Date:

Time:

Writing from:

What Goal did I work on today?

I am proud of myself today because:

I really did well at _____ today.

My goal for tomorrow is:

What did I learn today?

Other Notes:

I have faith in myself

Today's Date:

Time:

Writing from:

What Goal did I work on today?

I am proud of myself today because:

I really did well at _____ today.

My goal for tomorrow is:

What did I learn today?

Other Notes:

I have lots of energy

Today's Date:

Time:

Writing from:

What Goal did I work on today?

I am proud of myself today because:

I really did well at _____ **today.**

My goal for tomorrow is:

What did I learn today?

Other Notes:

I act responsibly

Today's Date:

Time:

Writing from:

What Goal did I work on today?

I am proud of myself today because:

I really did well at _____ today.

My goal for tomorrow is:

What did I learn today?

Other Notes:

I am peaceful

Today's Date:

Time:

Writing from:

What Goal did I work on today?

I am proud of myself today because:

I really did well at _____ today.

My goal for tomorrow is:

What did I learn today?

Other Notes:

I embrace change

Today's Date:

Time:

Writing from:

What Goal did I work on today?

I am proud of myself today because:

I really did well at _____ today.

My goal for tomorrow is:

What did I learn today?

Other Notes:

I make new friends easily

Today's Date:

Time:

Writing from:

What Goal did I work on today?

I am proud of myself today because:

I really did well at _____ today.

My goal for tomorrow is:

What did I learn today?

Other Notes:

I can become whatever I want to be

Today's Date:

Time:

Writing from:

What Goal did I work on today?

I am proud of myself today because:

I really did well at _____ today.

My goal for tomorrow is:

What did I learn today?

Other Notes:

I am joyful

Today's Date:

Time:

Writing from:

What Goal did I work on today?

I am proud of myself today because:

I really did well at _____ today.

My goal for tomorrow is:

What did I learn today?

Other Notes:

Life is fun

Today's Date:

Time:

Writing from:

What Goal did I work on today?

I am proud of myself today because:

I really did well at _____ today.

My goal for tomorrow is:

What did I learn today?

Other Notes:

I believe in miracles

Today's Date:

Time:

Writing from:

What Goal did I work on today?

I am proud of myself today because:

I really did well at _____ today.

My goal for tomorrow is:

What did I learn today?

Other Notes:

I am brave

Today's Date:

Time:

Writing from:

What Goal did I work on today?

I am proud of myself today because:

I really did well at _____ today.

My goal for tomorrow is:

What did I learn today?

Other Notes:

I am a good influence on others

Today's Date:

Time:

Writing from:

What Goal did I work on today?

I am proud of myself today because:

I really did well at _____ today.

My goal for tomorrow is:

What did I learn today?

Other Notes:

I am thoughtful

Today's Date:

Time:

Writing from:

What Goal did I work on today?

I am proud of myself today because:

I really did well at _____ today.

My goal for tomorrow is:

What did I learn today?

Other Notes:

I am confident

Today's Date:

Time:

Writing from:

What Goal did I work on today?

I am proud of myself today because:

I really did well at _____ today.

My goal for tomorrow is:

What did I learn today?

Other Notes:

I am a great student

Today's Date:

Time:

Writing from:

What Goal did I work on today?

I am proud of myself today because:

I really did well at _____ today.

My goal for tomorrow is:

What did I learn today?

Other Notes:

Others depend on me

Today's Date:

Time:

Writing from:

What Goal did I work on today?

I am proud of myself today because:

I really did well at _____ today.

My goal for tomorrow is:

What did I learn today?

Other Notes:

I take pride in myself

Today's Date:

Time:

Writing from:

What Goal did I work on today?

I am proud of myself today because:

I really did well at _____ today.

My goal for tomorrow is:

What did I learn today?

Other Notes:

I am dependable

Today's Date:

Time:

Writing from:

What Goal did I work on today?

I am proud of myself today because:

I really did well at _____ today.

My goal for tomorrow is:

What did I learn today?

Other Notes:

I am capable of so much

Today's Date:

Time:

Writing from:

What Goal did I work on today?

I am proud of myself today because:

I really did well at _____ today.

My goal for tomorrow is:

What did I learn today?

Other Notes:

I make a positive difference in the world

Today's Date:

Time:

Writing from:

What Goal did I work on today?

I am proud of myself today because:

I really did well at _____ today.

My goal for tomorrow is:

What did I learn today?

Other Notes:

I deserve to be respected

Today's Date:

Time:

Writing from:

What Goal did I work on today?

I am proud of myself today because:

I really did well at _____ today.

My goal for tomorrow is:

What did I learn today?

Other Notes:

Everything will be okay

Today's Date:

Time:

Writing from:

What Goal did I work on today?

I am proud of myself today because:

I really did well at _____ today.

My goal for tomorrow is:

What did I learn today?

Other Notes:

I accept who I am

Today's Date:

Time:

Writing from:

What Goal did I work on today?

I am proud of myself today because:

I really did well at _____ today.

My goal for tomorrow is:

What did I learn today?

Other Notes:

I make everyone around me better

Today's Date:

Time:

Writing from:

What Goal did I work on today?

I am proud of myself today because:

I really did well at _____ today.

My goal for tomorrow is:

What did I learn today?

Other Notes:

I am a product of my decisions

Today's Date:

Time:

Writing from:

What Goal did I work on today?

I am proud of myself today because:

I really did well at _____ today.

My goal for tomorrow is:

What did I learn today?

Other Notes:

Wonderful things await me

Today's Date:

Time:

Writing from:

What Goal did I work on today?

I am proud of myself today because:

I really did well at _____ today.

My goal for tomorrow is:

What did I learn today?

Other Notes:

My smile lights up a room

Today's Date:

Time:

Writing from:

What Goal did I work on today?

I am proud of myself today because:

I really did well at _____ **today.**

My goal for tomorrow is:

What did I learn today?

Other Notes:

When I fall, I am quick to get back up

Today's Date:

Time:

Writing from:

What Goal did I work on today?

I am proud of myself today because:

I really did well at _____ today.

My goal for tomorrow is:

What did I learn today?

Other Notes:

I nothing / no one defines who I am

Today's Date:

Time:

Writing from:

What Goal did I work on today?

I am proud of myself today because:

I really did well at _____ today.

My goal for tomorrow is:

What did I learn today?

Other Notes:

I have inner strength

Today's Date:

Time:

Writing from:

What Goal did I work on today?

I am proud of myself today because:

I really did well at _____ today.

My goal for tomorrow is:

What did I learn today?

Other Notes:

Success awaits me

Today's Date:

Time:

Writing from:

What Goal did I work on today?

I am proud of myself today because:

I really did well at _____ **today.**

My goal for tomorrow is:

What did I learn today?

Other Notes:

I've got this

Today's Date:

Time:

Writing from:

What Goal did I work on today?

I am proud of myself today because:

I really did well at _____ today.

My goal for tomorrow is:

What did I learn today?

Other Notes:

Today is a great day

Today's Date:

Time:

Writing from:

What Goal did I work on today?

I am proud of myself today because:

I really did well at _____ today.

My goal for tomorrow is:

What did I learn today?

Other Notes:

I am punctual

Today's Date:

Time:

Writing from:

What Goal did I work on today?

I am proud of myself today because:

I really did well at _____ today.

My goal for tomorrow is:

What did I learn today?

Other Notes:

My word is my bond

Today's Date:

Time:

Writing from:

What Goal did I work on today?

I am proud of myself today because:

I really did well at _____ **today.**

My goal for tomorrow is:

What did I learn today?

Other Notes:

I do everything to my fullest potential

Today's Date:

Time:

Writing from:

What Goal did I work on today?

I am proud of myself today because:

I really did well at _____ today.

My goal for tomorrow is:

What did I learn today?

Other Notes:

I believe in my dreams

Today's Date:

Time:

Writing from:

What Goal did I work on today?

I am proud of myself today because:

I really did well at _____ today.

My goal for tomorrow is:

What did I learn today?

Other Notes:

I inspire others to do better

Today's Date:

Time:

Writing from:

What Goal did I work on today?

I am proud of myself today because:

I really did well at _____ today.

My goal for tomorrow is:

What did I learn today?

Other Notes:

I have an excellent memory

Today's Date:

Time:

Writing from:

What Goal did I work on today?

I am proud of myself today because:

I really did well at _____ today.

My goal for tomorrow is:

What did I learn today?

Other Notes:

I start every day with a positive mindset

Today's Date:

Time:

Writing from:

What Goal did I work on today?

I am proud of myself today because:

I really did well at _____ today.

My goal for tomorrow is:

What did I learn today?

Other Notes:

I am emotionally healthy

Today's Date:

Time:

Writing from:

What Goal did I work on today?

I am proud of myself today because:

I really did well at _____ today.

My goal for tomorrow is:

What did I learn today?

Other Notes:

I take care of my physical health

Today's Date:

Time:

Writing from:

What Goal did I work on today?

I am proud of myself today because:

I really did well at _____ today.

My goal for tomorrow is:

What did I learn today?

Other Notes:

I am thoughful

Today's Date:

Time:

Writing from:

What Goal did I work on today?

I am proud of myself today because:

I really did well at _____ today.

My goal for tomorrow is:

What did I learn today?

Other Notes:

I am important

Today's Date:

Time:

Writing from:

What Goal did I work on today?

I am proud of myself today because:

I really did well at _____ **today.**

My goal for tomorrow is:

What did I learn today?

Other Notes:

I am intelligent

Today's Date:

Time:

Writing from:

What Goal did I work on today?

I am proud of myself today because:

I really did well at _____ today.

My goal for tomorrow is:

What did I learn today?

Other Notes:

I am an amazing person

Today's Date:

Time:

Writing from:

What Goal did I work on today?

I am proud of myself today because:

I really did well at _____ today.

My goal for tomorrow is:

What did I learn today?

Other Notes:

I become better everyday

Today's Date:

Time:

Writing from:

What Goal did I work on today?

I am proud of myself today because:

I really did well at _____ today.

My goal for tomorrow is:

What did I learn today?

Other Notes:

I control my happiness

Today's Date:

Time:

Writing from:

What Goal did I work on today?

I am proud of myself today because:

I really did well at _____ today.

My goal for tomorrow is:

What did I learn today?

Other Notes:

I make great choices

Today's Date:

Time:

Writing from:

What Goal did I work on today?

I am proud of myself today because:

I really did well at _____ today.

My goal for tomorrow is:

What did I learn today?

Other Notes:

My future looks bright

Today's Date:

Time:

Writing from:

What Goal did I work on today?

I am proud of myself today because:

I really did well at _____ today.

My goal for tomorrow is:

What did I learn today?

Other Notes:

I am working at my own pace

Today's Date:

Time:

Writing from:

What Goal did I work on today?

I am proud of myself today because:

I really did well at _____ today.

My goal for tomorrow is:

What did I learn today?

Other Notes:

Today I am going to shine

Today's Date:

Time:

Writing from:

What Goal did I work on today?

I am proud of myself today because:

I really did well at _____ today.

My goal for tomorrow is:

What did I learn today?

Other Notes:

My voice matters

Today's Date:

Time:

Writing from:

What Goal did I work on today?

I am proud of myself today because:

I really did well at _____ today.

My goal for tomorrow is:

What did I learn today?

Other Notes:

I am confident and secure

Today's Date:

Time:

Writing from:

What Goal did I work on today?

I am proud of myself today because:

I really did well at _____ today.

My goal for tomorrow is:

What did I learn today?

Other Notes:

Congratulations! You have completed an exercise that should be a daily habit throughout your life.

You matter, your life matters and it is important to have an intentional plan or ritual that ensures that you are reminding yourself of your great value every day – while speaking positive affirmations to yourself.

This discipline will reinforce the innate truth of your value while assisting you in setting goals and being intentional about becoming the best version of yourself that you were created to become.

You owe it to yourself to spend at least fifteen minutes a day to invest into your emotional wellbeing.

On the following page is a certificate, once you complete these exercises in their entirety please carefully remove the "certificate", fill it out and mail to the address provided to receive a <u>FREE gift</u>.

You matter, your life matters, and you were created to accomplish great things.

Blessings

Affirmation Goal Journal Certificate of Completion

Name: _Alivia Hendershot_

Address: _____

City: _____, State _____ Zip code: _____

1. Did you complete the <u>3</u> short-term goals?
2. Did you Complete the <u>3</u> long-term goals?
3. Did you complete all of the daily affirmation journal entries?
4. What was the most challenging part of the exercise?
5. Are you going to continue to set goals?
6. Are you going to continue reading daily affirmations to yourself?
7. Are you going to continue to process through your day by journaling?

Signature: _____ Date: _____

*Please mail via US Postal Service this form to John Hendershot c/o Affirmation Goal Journal. 72 W. 33rd Street, Holland, Michigan 49423

Made in the USA
Middletown, DE
29 June 2019